George Telfer

P

ZOOM IN ON

PHARAOHS OF EGYPT

ADAPTED BY
ANNE MILLARD

KING*f*ISHER

Contents

Anecdotes

Information

A Game

Information

A Test

Stickers

Postcards

The Prince's Strange Dream

Dangerous threats

*O*n that morning, the gazelles seemed to be reluctant to come and drink at the Nile's blue waters. Scanning the deserted horizon one last time, Egypt's young prince decided that it was useless to prolong his hunting party any longer. He put away his bow in its red leather holster and set off in his chariot at speed in the direction of Memphis, the capital city. The sound of the vigorous clicking of reins carried as far as the banks of the sacred river, where a

4

group of wild geese, nesting in a clump of papyrus, clattered into the air and flew off. The prince watched perplexed as they fled in full flight.

"What wouldn't I give to see the Bedouins, who are harassing the boundaries of the kingdom, clear off in the same way!" he thought.

A deep sense of weariness suddenly washed over him. For more than four months now, the army had been trying to put a stop to the incessant Bedouin attacks in the southwest of the country. But none of the forces had been able to drive back the assaults from the fierce desert nomads. Neither the knights nor the infantrymen had succeeded! Nor even the famous royal archers, despite their famed skills!

"Each day, Egypt is sinking a little further into chaos," the young prince said to himself, whilst guiding his horses. "Disorder is reigning instead of the rule of Ma'at, the goddess of truth and justice."

This confession of powerlessness made him shiver with terror. His heart began to race. Suddenly his head was spinning and his legs felt like jelly. He pulled clumsily on the reins, and his horses ground to a halt a few yards further on. The young prince got off his

chariot and staggered as best he could
towards the only visible group of rocks.

"The coolness in this little shaded circle of rocks
will set me back on my feet in no time at all," he
said to himself.

However, scarcely had he sat down when he felt
an invisible force closing his eyelids. He fell into a
deep sleep.

A message from the gods

While he was asleep, the young prince had a
terrible dream. When he woke up, he was so
distraught that he hastened back to the palace and
immediately summoned the three best magicians.
Dressed in their long white linen robes, Rai, Pasar
and Oubaoney rushed from their quarters to the
Council Chamber. The young prince was waiting
for them, looking very serious.

"You require our services?" the three honourable
sages asked respectfully.

The prince signalled to them to sit down and
told them the details of his nightmare.

"I saw a great storm striking Egypt!" he explained
in a voice trembling with emotion. "A sea of sand
engulfed the palace in the space of a few minutes!
Just when I thought the wind was dropping, a
huge whirlwind came in from the desert and

headed straight for me, spinning round at a breathtaking speed. It was so powerful that it dug out an enormous crater in the middle of the dunes, right beside my shelter. Then, in a deafening roar, it spat into the air the millions of grains of sand that it had picked up on its way. The golden dust crossed the sky to form a gleaming arc around the blood-red sun, which roared like an angry lion."

The sages looked at one another in silence. This dream was certainly not a good premonition!

"As we all know," continued the prince, "dreams are messages sent from the gods. This storm terrifies me! It makes me think of those incessant Bedouin attacks. I fear that this dream foretells a massive invasion."

"A consultation of the Book of Dreams will perhaps help us to understand exactly what the gods meant," suggested Rai.

"Go and get it as quickly as you can, my friend!" the prince said. "These are serious times!"

The Book of Dreams

"Let us proceed to the interpretation of your dream," began Rai, unrolling a lengthy papyrus covered in coloured hieroglyphs.

"Here is the first question," said Pasar. "Before the storm came, had you dreamt that you had

eaten any cucumbers?"

"Cucumbers? What a strange idea! No, I hadn't eaten any cucumbers."

"Good," said Pasar. "We can therefore eliminate immediately the announcement of a dispute with the king of Hyksos."

"When you speak of the roaring of the sun, would it not have been more like the mewing of a large cat?" asked Oubaoney.

"Certainly not!" replied the prince indignantly. "I know the difference between a lion and a cat."

"That's what I feared then," said Oubaoney. "The sender of this dream must be Re, the god of the sun, whose flames can devour flesh as quickly as the teeth of a wildcat. To go red like this, I am afraid that he has been angered."

"But why?" asked the prince. "I make sure that each morning I renew His creative force on Earth by practising the appropriate sacred rituals!"

"One last question," interrupted Rai. "From which direction did the sand come?"

"From the southwest, without any doubt," replied the prince.

"Hum!" said the sage, shaking his head. "Your fears are well-founded: the storm came from the southwest like the Bedouins. It seems as if

A Story

Re has decided to let Egypt be invaded by the Bedouins because He is angry, as Oubaoney suggests. Now we are getting somewhere! But we still have to identify the reason for His wrath so that we can appease Him before it is too late."

"I've got an idea!" exclaimed Pasar. "What if the crater formed by the whirlwind was a sign to show us that it was an important site – the site of a monument buried in sand, for example?"

"Why not!" exclaimed the prince. "It's true that the gods can't bear their temples and statues being poorly maintained or left abandoned. Let's go and examine the site!"

The secret of the dunes

On seeing the group of rocks where the prince had sheltered and slept, the magicians suspected immediately that it was the tip of an important edifice.

"It's a pyramid!" asserted Pasar, very sure of himself.

"You haven't a clue," said Oubaoney indignantly. "This rounded shape could only belong to a temple."

"Do you think so?" exclaimed Rai, in turn. "It

could only be the curve of a sacred vase."

Burning with impatience, the prince ordered his retinue to free the base of the block. But the task proved so enormous that the young prince was obliged to bring in five hundred extra workmen.

After three days of relentless work, a head wearing the royal scarf at last emerged from the sand. The prince was immediately dazzled by the purity of its features: its huge eyes stretched out like the setting sun; its fine nose was gracefully striking; and its smiling lips seemed to give out a message of love to the entire kingdom!

"Only the gods can give man the power to sculpt such a beautiful face!" marvelled the young prince.

In the following days, work did not cease until the statue's body was uncovered. When the workmen at last laid down their tools, the prince let out a cry of amazement "It's a Sphinx! Look!" he shouted to the magicians, who were just as fascinated as he by the size and beauty of the monument. "It's a giant Sphinx!"

The huge body of a lion stretched out for more than fifty metres. Protector of the good, this half-king, half-lion statue could once again look over the Nile in all its splendour. And as if by a miracle, barely twenty-four hours later, the army at last managed to defeat the fierce Bedouins! The prince at last became king and Egypt lived in peace again.

Never again did Re show anger towards the new king, who employed thirty men from his personal guard to undertake the daily upkeep of the Sphinx. As the ultimate homage to the god of Creation, he ordered that, at the foot of the statue, a stone stela be placed with the story of his adventure engraved on it.

The Gift of the

When drought hit the grasslands of the Sahara, its people, who were hunters and gatherers, were drawn to the well-watered Nile Valley. They settled there for good, and by 5000 BC had become farmers.

| 3200 BC | | 2780 BC | OLD KINGDOM | 2260 BC | 2050 BC | MIDDLE KINGDOM | 1785 |

The first dynasties (royal families)

Zoser   Khufu   Pepi   Mentuhotep   Sesostris

Nile

■ Surrounded by desert

In a land where it hardly rains, the Nile supplies
all of Egypt's water – without it there would be
only desert. For four months each year the Nile
floods, bringing water and fertile mud to the
fields. The farmers dug canals to control the
floodwater.

■ A united nation

The settlers prospered, and states began to emerge.
In time, two states became more powerful than the
others. Then, in about 3100 BC Menes, King of
Upper Egypt (the Nile Valley), conquered Lower
Egypt (the Delta).

■ Pharaoh

The king's title was King of Upper and Lower
Egypt. Pharaoh was a later title. It comes from two
ancient Egyptian words meaning 'great house' or
palace. It was a respectful way to refer to the king.

■ Absolute power

The king of Egypt was a god on earth. He owned the land and made all the
decisions. From his palace in Memphis he controlled the lives of all his subjects.
But he ruled wisely and with justice, in accordance with the wishes of the gods.

80 BC	NEW KINGDOM		1085 BC	332 BC	GREEK EMPIRE	30 BC	ROMAN EMPIRE
nenhotep	*Tuthmosis*	*Rameses*		*Alexander*	*Cleopatra*		

The Importance of

In about 2800 BC, the Old Kingdom began. One of Egypt's greatest ages, it is also known as the Pyramid Age.

Egyptian society was like a pyramid, with the king at the top. Then came scribes, priests and officials, followed by servants and craftworkers.

■ Hundreds of scribes

The pharaoh had ministers to help him govern, and orders were recorded and carried out by an army of scribes. They made notes on flakes of limestone or bits of broken pottery. Proper documents were written on papyrus, a kind of paper.

■ Writing: the key to success

The Egyptians invented the picture writing we call hieroglyphics. To get a government job, you had to be able to read and write. Many parents struggled to pay for a son's education. School could be tough – teachers were told to beat lazy pupils. But it was worth it, for a scribe had a good life.

the Scribes

■ What are hieroglyphs?

Some hieroglyphs express an idea: a picture of the
sun can mean 'the sun'. Some pictures also stand
for a sound: a picture of the mouth is a mouth,
but it is also the sound 'r'. These
sound signs build up words.
Other signs go at the end of a
word. They have no sound but
help us to understand the
word. For example, a pair of
walking legs indicates movement.

■ Thousands of texts

In Egypt, scribes recorded everything: the orders
given and the reports that the tasks were done.
They noted the height of the flood water each
year and how much gold was mined. Records
were kept of business deals and wills, of trials
and taxes. Even the number of wicks used
in lamps by the royal tomb-builders was
noted! Thanks to his scribes, the
pharaoh held the entire kingdom
under his sway.

*A scribe's
palette and brushes*

The King and

Early royal tombs were *mastabas*, built of mud bricks. In Dynasty III, the Egyptians began building stone pyramids.

◼ Imhotep the Wise

Imhotep was a courtier, a top government official, the high priest of the sun-god Re (or Ra), and an architect. He designed and built the world's first pyramid, the step pyramid at Sakkara. He is also said to have been a doctor and to have reformed the writing system and the calendar. No wonder he was later revered as a god!

A mastaba was a rectangular tomb with sloping sides. The first pyramid was made by adding steps on top.

the Genius

■ The step pyramid

Imhotep designed the step pyramid to be King Zoser's tomb.
It has six steps, once covered in blocks of white limestone.
Did Imhotep design it as a stairway which the king's
spirit could climb to join the gods?

■ Make-believe buildings

The step pyramid is surrounded by buildings
inside a great enclosure wall. The pyramid is thought
to represent the palace in its walled courtyard. The other
buildings represent the offices and storerooms of the palace.
But the buildings are solid, without any rooms. They are
magic, for use by spirits, not by the living. There is also a
courtyard where Zoser can go on holding the magic Heb Sed
festival, which will renew his strength forever.

■ The king's crowns

The White Crown of Upper Egypt and the Red
Crown of Lower Egypt were worn together as the
Double Crown, symbolizing the union of the Two
Lands. The Blue Crown, or war helmet, was worn
by the kings of the New Kingdom. The serpent
protected the king from his enemies.

Working in Stone

Egypt had an abundance of building material – yellow sandstone, pink granite, white limestone and alabaster, as well as semi-precious stones.

Manpower

In Ancient Egypt, people did not use money. Taxes were paid to the king in goods and in labour. The men who built the pyramids and did the hard work in quarries and mines were not slaves but free men – peasants paying their taxes! When the Nile was in flood they could not work in the fields, so the king employed, housed, fed and clothed them.

■ Stone quarrying

Masons used copper chisels to cut holes in rock, outlining each block to be taken. Other workers drove wooden pegs into the holes with mallets. The pegs were soaked with water and swelled up, splitting the block away from the rock-face.

■ Gliding on sand

The blocks were put onto sledges and tied on with ropes. Men hauled on the ropes and dragged the sledges over the sand. To make the sledges move more easily, a team of men went in front, putting down a path of rollers. To stop the friction causing a fire, other men poured water over the rollers.

■ Floating on the Nile

The blocks were stored at the quarry until the Nile was in flood. Then they were put on barges and floated to the building site. This was far easier than a long journey over land.

■ An annual task

The whole process was repeated year after year for the pharaohs' building projects. Once on site, the blocks were shaped to an exact fit. Using only copper tools and hard stones as grinders and polishers, the early Egyptians produced amazing results!

Khufu's Great Pyramid

*About 2,300,000 blocks of
stone were used to build the
Great Pyramid. Each one
weighed about 2.5 tonnes.*

In about 2700 BC, King Khufu ordered the building of a huge
pyramid. It is the largest ever built in Egypt – but the only
statuette of the king to survive is a tiny one made of ivory.
Perhaps his gods had a sense of humour!

◼ The Great Pyramid

Khufu's pyramid was straight-sided. Religious writings called
the Pyramid Texts speak of the king climbing up to the sun-
god on ramps of sunbeams. Perhaps the straight sides of the
pyramid were supposed to be those ramps. Khufu's pyramid
stood 147 m high and was encased in blocks of white
limestone. How dazzling it must have looked in the sun!

Information

■ The pyramid's treasures

All that now remains in Khufu's pyramid is the plain granite sarcophagus (stone coffin) intended to protect his body from decay and thieves. The magnificent treasures buried with him to take to the Next World have all been stolen.

Embalming involved covering the body with salt to remove fluids and prevent decay.

■ Pyramid temples

Khufu's body was probably *embalmed* and made into a mummy on the roof of the Valley Temple. A causeway links the Valley Temple to the Mortuary Temple, where priests made offerings to the king's spirit each day. Their prayers and offerings were supposed to be made for all eternity.

Tomb robbers stole all the treasures from all the pyramids, including Khufu's.

■ Khufu's royal fleet

Everyone, kings and commoners alike, travelled by boat. Even the sun-god sailed across the sky! So Khufu had great pits dug near his pyramid. A fleet of boats was dismantled and put in the pits. Only two have survived, one of which has been rebuilt. What a jigsaw it was! But everything was there - planks, ropes and oars. The boat is 23 m long.

An Activity

What a Puzzle this

During the Old and Middle Kingdoms – that is, for nearly 1,200 years – the kings (and some of their queens) were buried in pyramids. Those built in Dynasty IV are the biggest and best. Middle Kingdom pyramids were built of mud-brick with stone casing. A pyramid was built to guard a king's mummified body and treasures. It was a magic place to help launch his spirit to join the gods. It was also the place where daily offerings were made to his spirit.

You will need:
• a sheet of strong paper
• a pair of compasses
• a ruler and pencil
• scissors
• glue

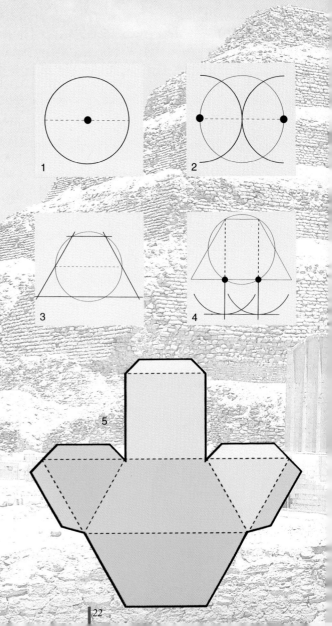

An Activity

Pyramid is!

To build the pyramid you must make it in two parts.
1. Reproduce the drawing with the compasses set at 2.5 cm, following steps A to D.
2. Make the folding tabs and mark out the dotted lines (step E).
3. Score the folding lines with the point of the scissors to make folding easier.
4. Cut out the pieces. Fold and glue them together. Now try fitting them together to make the pyramid.

The solution is on p.63.

On Foot or by Boat

The Nile was Egypt's main road!
The easiest way to travel through
Egypt was by boat. Small boats
were made of reeds, the rest were
made of wood. If you had to travel
over land, you went on foot.
Donkeys were used to carry loads,
not people.

◼ Carried in splendour

The pharaohs and their nobles did not walk. They were carried by their servants
in special carrying chairs. The king's carrying chair was made of expensive
foreign wood, covered with gold foil and inlaid with semi-precious stones.
Servants with ostrich-feather fans kept him cool and one carried his sandals.

Information

■ Oars and sails

Egyptian ships were made of wooden planks, held together by wooden pegs and ropes. When they reached a cataract – a place where rocks filled the river-bed and blocked the path of ships – they could easily be taken apart and

assembled again. To go downstream (north) the sailors had to row. To go upstream (south) they used a sail, because the wind usually blew from north to south.

■ Royal ships

Kings regularly made tours of inspection through Egypt. Pictures and models show the king's ship was brightly painted. There was a cabin to sleep in at night, but by day he could sit on deck in a cushioned armchair, sheltered from the sun by a gauze awning as he nibbled honey cakes and sipped wine.

A Time of

The Old Kingdom ended with the breakdown of government and increasing lawlessness and despair. Historians call this the First Intermediate Period.

■ Chaos!

About 2260 BC the heirs of King Pepi II lost control of Egypt. Libyans and Asiatics invaded and the country was split by civil war and disorder. Brigands roamed the land. Peasants felt it was no use planting crops because they would be stolen. Famine was widespread and fear reigned.

Despair

■ The nomarchs

The nomarchs were noblemen who ran the districts
into which Egypt was divided. They passed their offices
on from father to son. They had been steadily increasing
their power at the expense of the king's. Now they went
farther. They claimed rights that had once belonged only
to royalty and set themselves up as little kings within their own
districts, with armies to guard them.

■ Egypt divided

"Seventy kings in seventy days" was how the
Egyptians later described the free-for-all when the
nomarchs were in power. Then the nomarchs of
Herakleopolis claimed to be pharaohs of the entire
land. They were bitterly opposed by the nomarchs of
Thebes, a province in the south. The victor in the war
was Mentuhotep of Thebes.

■ Artists in decline

In the Old Kingdom, the very best craftsmen
had worked in the royal workshops attached to
the palace at Memphis. They produced statues
that rank among the world's greatest
masterpieces. Other craftsmen made
lovely jewellery, furniture and stone
vessels. When royal government
collapsed, the craftsmen and artists
attached themselves to the
nomarchs' courts but without royal
support standards declined.

The Middle Kingdom

In about 2050 BC, King Mentuhotep reunited the Two Lands. This is the beginning of the Middle Kingdom, a second Golden Age. It lasted about 300 years. Art and learning flourished.

◼ The return of order

Mentuhotep moved the capital from Memphis to Thebes and set about restoring royal power, Egypt's wealth and its influence abroad. His dynasty was followed by an even greater one – that of kings Amenemhat and Senusret. The Libyans were beaten. The northern part of Nubia, up to the Second Cataract, became an Egyptian province. Trade flourished with Sinai and Asiatic cities like Byblos.

Boats returned from Nubia loaded with gold, ivory, ebony, incense and strange animals such as monkeys and leopards.

No more nomarchs

The new kings did not forget how the nomarchs had caused the decline of the Old Kingdom. To make sure it did not happen again, Senusret III did away with the office of nomarch. He divided Egypt into three regions, run by loyal officials.

Egypt looks outwards

The pharaohs sent expeditions into the deserts around Egypt to look for gold, copper, jewels and stones for building. They also sent ships over the sea to the land of Punt, source of the highly-prized incense. Punt was probably southeast of Egypt, in modern Somalia.

Golden age

Wealth flowed into Egypt to finance the revival of art and learning and the construction of temples, forts and pyramids. Much has been destroyed, but what survives shows how magnificent the Middle Kingdom was.

Soldiers and

The pharaoh's army ensured that the order established throughout the kingdom was respected by its inhabitants and by neighbouring countries.

■ Pharaoh as warrior hero

Old Kingdom kings were thought to be too holy to lead an army, but in the Middle Kingdom several kings led their troops. One of the greatest warriors was Senusret I. He looked magnificent as he reviewed his soldiers, with the serpent *Uraeus* shining on his forehead. "He is a brave man... a man of action without equal," wrote one scribe.

The Uraeus was the serpent that kings wore on the front of their crowns. It protected them by spitting fire at their enemies.

■ Good soldiers

Egyptian soldiers were well-trained. In battle, trumpets sounded to tell them where to move. They could use spears, swords, daggers, axes, bows and arrows, and battle maces. They wore no armour, not even a helmet, but they did have large shields made of wood and leather. They used battering rams and scaling ladders when they besieged enemy cities and fortresses.

Fortresses

■ Fortresses and death curses

To protect their southern and eastern frontiers, the Egyptians built massive fortresses of mud bricks. These were as impenetrable as any medieval castle. As a second line of defence, priest-magicians made clay figures of foreign enemy princes, wrote their names on them and put spells on them. If an enemy attacked, his figure was smashed and he would be destroyed by the magic.

Pharaoh's Peasants

Egyptian peasants waged eternal warfare with the deserts, using the waters of the Nile flood to keep the sands at bay. Every inch of land that would grow crops was precious. So villages were small and the dead were buried in the desert.

■ Sow in mud, then water...

The moment the waters of the Nile flood went down, the peasants were out in their muddy fields. Simple hoes broke up large clods of earth, then oxen pulled ploughs across the ground. Seeds for wheat, barley, flax and vegetables were cast over the soil. Sheep were then driven across the fields, to push the seeds into the ground with their hooves. Next came the hard work – watering, weeding and scaring birds away.

■ The harvest

At harvest time the reapers, armed with sickles, cut the grain stalks to the rhythm of a flute-player. The sheaves were carried to the threshing floor in baskets on a donkey's back, and cows were driven round and round to separate the grain from the straw. Women then winnowed the grain by tossing it in the air so the lighter husks blew away, leaving the precious grain ready for storage.

■ Horrible hippos!

A swarm of hungry locusts could eat a whole crop. After that, hippos were a farmer's worst enemy. If one rolled in your field, it flattened anything growing there!

Information

1. The field was ploughed, then the wheat was sown by hand.

3. The straw was separated from the grain.

4. A scribe was there to see that taxes were paid!

■ Royal taxes

A royal scribe inspected the growing crop and told each farmer how many sacks of grain he must pay in taxes. Taxes went to the royal granaries and the farmer stored the rest to feed his family. After the harvest, the irrigation canals had to be cleaned and repaired. Then the farmer might have to work for the pharaoh for four months before going back to his fields.

2. The shaduf raised water for the crops.

An Ancient Game

The Egyptians were very fond of games. Archaeologists have found magnificent gaming boards in some tombs, made of ebony, ivory and gold. The favourite game was called senet. Another was hounds and jackals. You can make the ancient game of mancala using an egg-box and some hard white haricot beans.

You will need:
- an empty egg-box for 12 eggs
- 48 dried beans
- paints and brush
- a knife

To make your mancala game:
1. Cut the top off the egg-box.
2. Paint the bottom part of the box yellow on the inside and blue on the outside.
3. With a fine brush paint Egyptian motifs in dark red and blue. Use the picture to help you.

An Activity

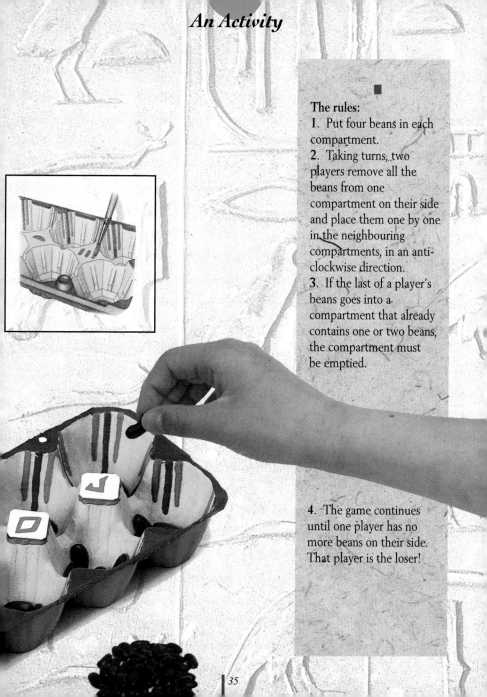

The rules:
1. Put four beans in each compartment.
2. Taking turns, two players remove all the beans from one compartment on their side and place them one by one in the neighbouring compartments, in an anti-clockwise direction.
3. If the last of a player's beans goes into a compartment that already contains one or two beans, the compartment must be emptied.

4. The game continues until one player has no more beans on their side. That player is the loser!

Pharaoh as Hunter

The marshes along the banks of the Nile provided birds
and fish for food. But they were also the home of man-
eating hippos and crocodiles. Getting rid of them was
the sport of kings and nobles.

Information

■ Humble shepherds

Egypt's fertile land was used to grow crops. There was little land to spare for pasture, so shepherds and herdsmen grazed their animals on the banks of the river and in the marshes, where the valuable animals could feed well.

■ Birds galore

The marshes were home to countless water birds. Bird-catchers trapped the birds in nets to sell in the market. But for the nobles and kings, catching birds with throwing-sticks was a sport, not a livelihood.

■ Going fishing

The river teemed with fish of many kinds. Morning and evening, the fishermen were out in their reed boats catching fresh fish to sell. They used nets and lines with several hooks on the end, then quickly clubbed the fish they landed. Fish that were not sold immediately were dried so that they would keep. Kings and nobles went on fishing trips using harpoons.

■ Sport or ritual?

For the people who worked in the marshes, crocodiles and hippos were dangerous beasts that had to be exterminated. In ancient Egyptian religion, male hippos were a symbol of evil. So pharaohs and nobles enjoyed special hippo hunts that were also a religious ritual, designed to drive evil from the land.

The Foreign Conquerors

The Middle Kingdom collapsed in civil war and foreign invasions. From about 1680 to 1580 BC Egypt was ruled by foreigners.

■ The hated invaders

The Hyksos came from over the eastern frontier. The name comes from two ancient Egyptian words meaning 'rulers of foreign hill-countries'. The Egyptians never forgot the shock and humiliation of being defeated and ruled by these Asiatic invaders. The Hyksos were remembered as cruel barbarians who killed and destroyed.

■ Order imposed by the Hyksos

The Hyksos ruled the Delta from their capital at Avaris. Middle Egypt was ruled by Egyptians who were vassals of the Hyksos. The South was independent, but had to pay tribute to the Hyksos.

■ More Egyptian than the Egyptians?

Though the Egyptians later claimed the Hyksos were vile, evil men, who 'ruled without Re' (the Egyptian sun-god), in fact they quickly adopted the culture, religion and learning of their Egyptian subjects. They used the Egyptian language and hieroglyphs and encouraged the copying of old texts. They adopted Egyptian names, titles and customs. But to the Egyptians they were still hated foreigners.

Information

■ Secret weapon!

One reason why the Hyksos beat the Egyptians so easily was that they had horses and chariots, unknown in Egypt until then. The

Egyptians quickly adopted the new weapon. How wonderful it must have felt, charging across the desert at speeds undreamed of, or riding down a street and towering above poor people on foot!

Houses were built of mud bricks and had flat roofs.

Amenhotep

In about 1580 BC Amosis, the ruler of Thebes, led the revolt that drove out the Hyksos. ~~~~~~ start of the New King~~~~~ 's empire.

Priests making offerings to the god Amun

and Tuthmosis

Tuthmosis

■ Warrior pharaohs

Two kings named Amenhotep (I and II) and two named
Tuthmosis (I and III) were the greatest warrior pharaohs in
Egypt's history. They conquered the greatest empire of the day,
stretching from the Fourth Cataract of the Nile as far as the
Euphrates River. Trading links were wider than ever before, and
subject peoples sent tribute every year.

Amenhotep I

■ Magnificent temples

The warrior pharaohs believed that Amun (the local god of
Thebes, whose sacred animal was a ram) had given them
their victories. They made him king of the gods and built
him vast temples with halls of tall columns, huge statues
and obelisks. They gave him presents – vessels of gold and
silver, jewels and many prisoners of war as slaves. Other gods
and goddesses also benefited from the empire's wealth.

■ The Valley of the Kings

All the pyramids were robbed during Egypt's times of trouble, so the New
Kingdom pharaohs came up with another plan. Their tombs were cut into the
rock face of a valley on the west bank at Thebes – the famous Valley of the
Kings. A pyramid-shaped mountain looms over the valley.
The kings were buried with fabulous treasures.

■ The tomb of Tutankhamun

Tutankhamun was only ten when he came to the throne
and he reigned for just ten years. But he is the most famous
pharaoh of all, because his was the only tomb to survive
intact to the 20th century. A vast amount of treasure was
packed into his small tomb. What must have been in the
large tombs of important kings who reigned for many years?

Tutankhamun

Incredibl

THE INVENTION OF INCOME TAX

In about 650 BC the new pharaoh decreed that, each year, every Egyptian must report to a local official and reveal how much income they received. The amount of tax they had to pay was then calculated. Anyone who failed to report to the official, or who lied about their income, could face the death penalty!

STRANGE VASES

When the very ancient Egyptians made their first pots and stone vessels, they were living very simple lives. They spent most of their time outdoors, so they made pots and vases with pointed bottoms that could be driven into the sand to make them stand up. Hundreds of years later, they still made most of their pots with pointed bottoms. But to make them stand up in their houses, they had to use pot rings and stands! Large pots were used to store wine, grain and oil. Smaller ones might contain perfumes.

but True!

HOW TO COUNT DEAD ENEMIES

After a battle, Egyptian soldiers cut off the right hand of each dead enemy soldier and put them in a pile. This made it easier for the scribe in charge to count up the numbers of enemy dead!

CURIOUS CONES

When they were going to a banquet, men and women had cones of perfumed fat fixed to their hair. During the evening, as they got hot, the cones melted and the fat ran down their faces, cooling them and smelling delightful. For ceremonies and special occasions, men and women wore heavy wigs.

Rameses the Great

**During the New Kingdom, 11 of Egypt's pharaohs were named
Rameses. The most famous of them all is Rameses II, who reigned
for 67 years and had more than 100 children!**

▨ A propaganda artist

Rameses II understood the value of propaganda as
well as any modern politician. When he fought
against the Hittites at Kadesh, the result was a
draw. However, the story of his bravery was
recorded on the walls of temple after temple. He
told the gods and the people alike that it was a
magnificent victory!

■ The builder pharaoh

In his long reign, Rameses II had massive temples
built across Egypt and Nubia. These include the
wonderful temples cut into the cliff face at Abu
Simbel. He also built a new city, towns, palaces and
tombs for himself, his wives and children. All were
built on a grand scale. In addition, his name was
cut all over the monuments of former pharaohs,
claiming them for himself!

■ Water and peace

When Rameses learned that an expedition
crossing the desert had died of thirst, he ordered
his men to dig wells across the desert. This was a
tremendous undertaking, because the wells had to
be very deep. And as he had won back some of the
empire lost by a previous pharaoh, he also made
peace with the Hittites.

■ City of treasure

Rameses built the city of Pi-Rameses in the
Delta. Behind a high *palisade* were palaces for the
royal family and temples for the gods, all built on
a grand scale and full of treasures. There were
villas for the nobles and officials, and offices for
them to work in. There were also special quarters
for skilled craftsmen, as well as quays lined with
boatyards and storehouses for the merchants. Here,
it was said, even the poor could lead a good life.

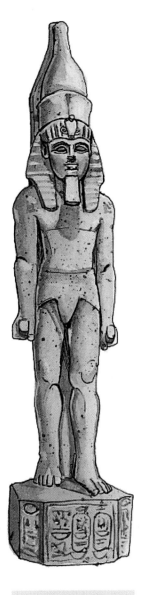

*A palisade is a high
wall built to protect a
city from invaders.*

The Tomb-makers' Village

The craftsmen who made the tombs of New Kingdom pharaohs and their queens were a very privileged group. They carried a huge responsibility and were rewarded accordingly.

■ Pampered workers

The men who built and painted the tombs of the New Kingdom pharaohs and their families lived together in a village specially built for them on the west bank at Thebes. They were among the highest paid craftsmen in Egypt.

■ The village of Deir el-Medina

Sixty stone masons and artists, together with their families, lived in the village that is now called Deir el-Medina. They had a wall to protect them from desert brigands and servants supplied by the king to grind grain and do heavy work. A temple was built to the north of the village and the men had enough free time to cut their own tombs in the cliff behind the village.

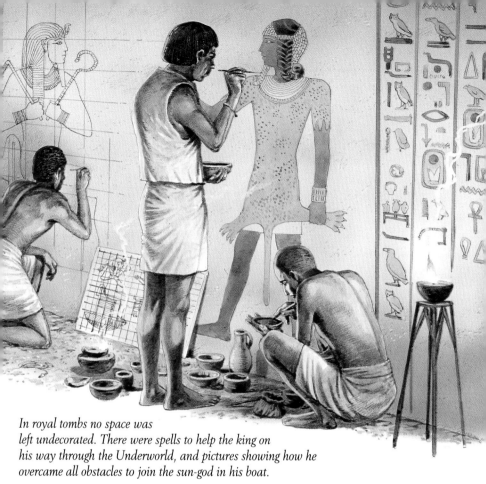

In royal tombs no space was left undecorated. There were spells to help the king on his way through the Underworld, and pictures showing how he overcame all obstacles to join the sun-god in his boat.

■ Good wages for good work

The workmen of the village had regular hours and holidays. They were paid in food and goods, and if the wages were late, they went on strike! In return they excavated the tomb in the rock, and smoothed and plastered the walls. Artists outlined the pictures and writing, then the most skilled ones made corrections and filled in details. The tombs were masterpieces, but destined to be seen only by the gods.

Danger – Men at Work!

A Game

Everyone is busy! But look carefully. Can you see anything strange? You should be able to find 20 mistakes in the picture.

Solution on p.63

Men of Learning

Thanks to the skills of the engineers, stonemasons, sculptors and artists, we can still marvel at the wonders of Ancient Egypt.

A pyramid had to be aligned with the Pole Star in the north.

Set square with plumb line

■ What was their secret?

The secret of Egyptian success was study, hard work and a talent for organizing the labour of large numbers of men. They used simple tools such as plumblines and copper chisels. Their techniques were based on using men, rollers, ropes and sand. And their scholars' calculations were exact.

Information

■ Stargazing

From the time they settled in the Nile Valley, the ancient Egyptians began studying the heavens. Thanks to the clear air, they could study the movements of stars and planets every night. They studied other natural phenomena too, such as the Nile's annual flood. They used their observations to create a calendar with 12 months of 30 days and 5 special days at the end. We owe our 365-day calendar to them. The 24-hour day was another of their discoveries.

■ Medicine and magic

The Egyptian doctors were excellent, and many of their treatments and medicines would have been effective. But they were very religious people, so they involved the gods in everything. A good medicine was even better if you said a prayer as you took it. Also, as they thought many illnesses were caused by 'hostile forces', it helped to wear magic amulets for protection.

Protective amulets (lucky charms)

A Troubled Age

After the death of the last Rameses, in about 1085 BC, Egypt entered a troubled time when the country was divided among rival pharaohs. Prices rose steeply, tomb robbers abounded and foreigners invaded.

■ The Libyan takeover

For many years, the pharaohs employed Libyan soldiers in their armies. They were given land and allowed to settle. They adopted Egyptian ways and some of their leaders became top government officials. In about 950 BC one of them, Sheshonq, was crowned pharaoh. The first Libyan kings were strong rulers, but then quarrels broke out in the royal family and the country split into four kingdoms and several princedoms.

Information

■ One invasion after another

At the end of the New Kingdom, Nubia and *Kush* broke away and became an independent kingdom with its own king. In about 750 BC the Nubians invaded and conquered Egypt and ruled as pharaohs. Their success was short-lived. The Assyrians invaded Egypt and drove out the Nubian royal family. In 665 BC they sacked the holy city of Thebes and used native Egyptian princes to rule for them.

Kush is in modern-day Sudan, which lies to the south of Egypt.

■ To the rescue!

One of the princes chosen by the Assyrians to rule Egypt for them was Psamtek of Sais. He stopped paying tribute to the Assyrians and became pharaoh of a united Egypt. His dynasty brought peace and prosperity, revived Egypt's art and restored its greatness. But then yet more enemies arrived – the Persians.

The temple at Edfu

Persians and Greeks

For nearly 200 years, the Egyptians suffered under Persian rule. Freedom fighters struggled against the Persians and managed to drive them out, but they returned. Then the Greeks arrived.

The Pharos (lighthouse) of Alexandria

Information

■ Beware of the Persians!

In 525 BC the Persians conquered Egypt. The Egyptians hated being just another province of the Persian Empire and many resistance groups held out – especially in the Delta – and they won! Egypt was independent for a while, then the Persians returned.

■ Alexander the Great

Alexander, king of Macedonia, conquered the Persian Empire province by province. The Egyptians loathed the Persians, so when Alexander arrived in 332 BC he was hailed as a deliverer and accepted as a pharaoh sent to them by the gods. He stayed only a few months, then left in search of new conquests.

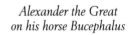

Alexander the Great on his horse Bucephalus

■ Alexandria

During his short time in Egypt, Alexander ordered the building of a new capital, which was named after him. Alexandria had a magnificent harbour and lighthouse. It became a great centre of learning and culture.

■ The Ptolemies

After the death of Alexander, his generals fought each other for control of the empire. Ptolemy seized and held on to Egypt, establishing the line of kings all called Ptolemy. The Egyptians resented the way all the top positions in government went to Greeks. But the firm control and efficiency of the early Ptolemies restored Egypt's prosperity, and they built many temples to the Egyptian gods.

The Last Pharaoh

While the Greeks and Egyptians learned to live together, new storm clouds gathered. Rome had its eye on the wealth and grain of the East.

■ Family feuds

Sadly, as a family the Ptolemies were a disaster. Brothers and sisters, mothers and sons, struggled for power and often murdered one another. Cleopatra VII came to the throne in 50 BC with the help of the Roman leader Julius Caesar.

Octavian, Roman general and emperor

■ The gifted queen

Cleopatra was a clever woman and a good ruler, who dreamed of using Roman power to restore Egypt's lost empire. But she supported the wrong man in the struggle for power between Octavian and Mark Anthony, joint rulers of the Roman world. Octavian declared war on Antony and Cleopatra and defeated them at the battle of Actium in 31 BC. Cleopatra committed suicide rather than be taken prisoner by Octavian.

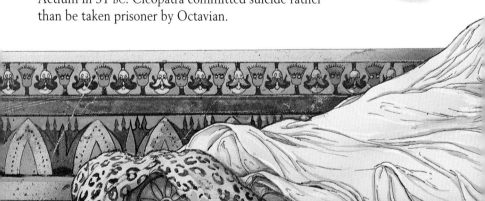

■ A Roman triumph

In 30 BC, Egypt became a province in
Rome's rapidly growing empire. It was an
important province, because much of
the grain that Rome needed to feed its
citizens came from there. But the days
of Egypt's independence and glory were
over. There would never be another
pharaoh.

*Cleopatra used a
poisonous snake to
commit suicide.*

■ The pharaohs loved horse-riding in the desert.

False: Ancient Egyptians used their horses to pull their chariots. Only a few army scouts may have ridden horses.

☐ The Ancient Egyptians wore make-up.

True. Both sexes used cosmetics. The most important items in a cosmetic box were the oils used to stop the skin drying up in the sun.

■ Egypt has always been ruled by Egyptian pharaohs.

False: There were foreign pharaohs – Hyksos, Libyans, Nubians and Greeks.

☐ Royal tomb builders were killed to protect the tomb.

False: The workers lived comfortably in their village. No one was killed. They served one king after the other.

☐ Rameses II won a great military victory at Kadesh in Asia.

False: Rameses II managed to prevent a disaster, but he did not take Kadesh.

False?

If a pharaoh had a hole in a tooth, his doctor could cure it.

True: The Egyptians were good dentists as well as doctors. A hole in the tooth might be sealed with a mineral cement.

Building a royal tomb took less than a year.

False: Tombs in the Valley of the Kings took several years to complete.

The Roman general Octavian killed Queen Cleopatra.

False: Cleopatra killed herself by making a poisonous snake bite her.

Tutankhamun lived to a great age and had lots of children.

False: He died when he was only 20 years old.

The Egyptians liked locusts.

Egyptian scholars invented our calendar.

True: They invented a 365-day calendar on which ours is based.

The Egyptians painted their eyes for medical reasons.

True: Besides making the eyes look big and beautiful, galena (a black powder ground up and mixed with oil) will keep flies out of the eyes and so protect them from disease.

Alexander the Great grew old in Egypt and died there.

False: He only stayed a few months before departing for more conquests. He died in Babylon in 323 BC, aged 67 years.

False: They dreaded them. A swarm of locusts can eat a field of grain in a few hours.

False?

Memphis was the only capital of Egypt.

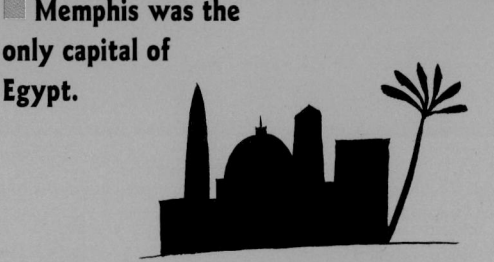

False: There have been other capitals – Thebes, It-towy, Tell el Amarna, Sais, Alexandria and Cairo.

The Egyptian alphabet has 26 letters.

False: The Egyptians did not have an alphabet. There were over 700 hieroglyphic signs. Some were worth one letter, others two, three or four.

The Egyptians liked to be overweight.

True: A well-covered body was a sign of wealth and success.

The greatest pyramids belonged to the last pharaohs.

False: The greatest pyramids were built during Dynasty IV in the Old Kingdom.

Index

Solution to the game on pages 22-23

Both parts of the pyramid have a square side – place them together.

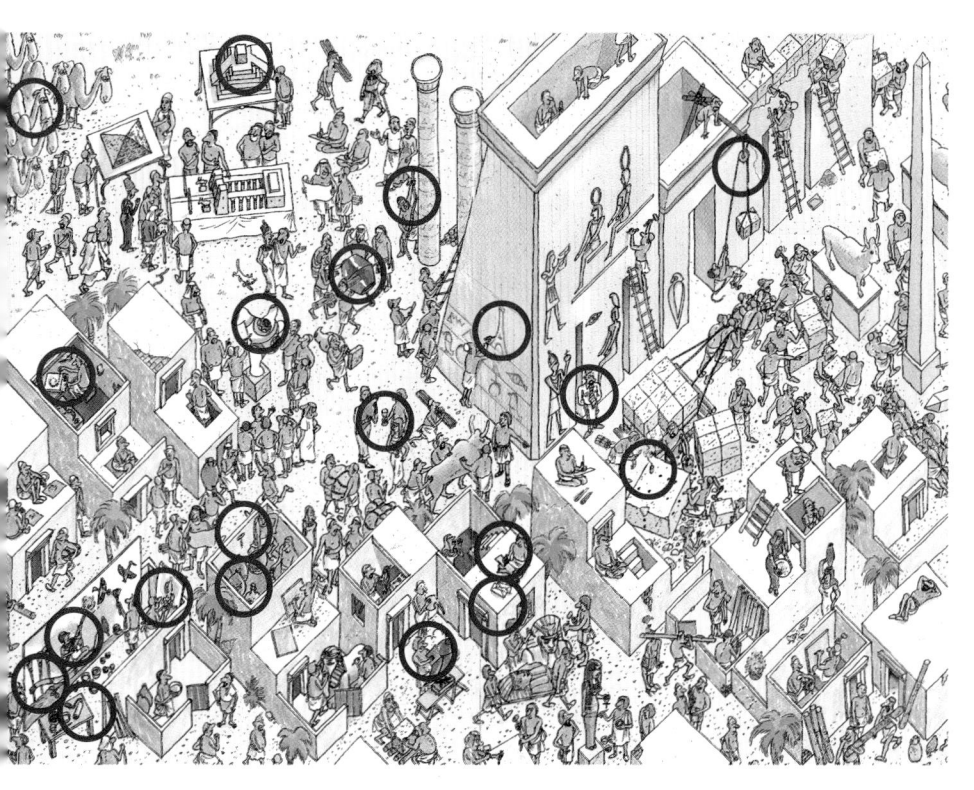

Solution to the game on pages 48-49

You should have found the camel train (unknown in ancient Egypt), the electronic scales (a 20th century invention, the gun (a mid-14th century invention), the motor propeller (a 19th century invention), the Mayan temple (1st century AD, in Central America), the modern paint brush, the paint roller, the modern sculpture, the bottle opener (a 17th century invention), the jar with the flat base (most Egyptian jars had pointed bases), the cement mixer (20th century), the folding ruler (a 17th century invention), the transparent glass (you could not see through Egyptian glass), sandpaper (a 20th century invention), the Eiffel Tower (built between 1887 and 1889), the modern pen and envelope, the tie and shirt, the stick of dynamite (a 19th century invention), the pulley block (4th century BC).

Created by Marie-Odile Fordacq
Authors Claire Derouin, Béatrice Garel, Viviane Koenig, Catherine Pauwel
Managing editors Marie-Odile Fordacq, Camilla Hallinan
Editorial co-ordinators Ariane Léandri, Molly Perham
Art editors Sue Aldworth, Ch'en Ling, Bernard Girodroux, Val Pidgeon, Val Wright
Illustrators Ian Chamberlain, Peter Dennis, Francesca D'Ottavi, Jeff Fisher,
Chris Forsey, Lynda Gray, Daniel Guerrier, Nick Hall, Nicki Palin, Richard Ward
Photo research Veneta Bullen
Photo credits AKG London, Ancient Art and Architecture, Bridgeman Art Library
(British Museum; Giraudon; Louvre, Paris), BBC Natural History Unit, British Museum,
Brooklyn Museum of Art, Peter Clayton, Robert Harding, Mansell Collection,
Tim Ridley Photography, The Stockmarket / Zefa, Werner Forman
Design and page make-up équipage, Olivier Lemoine,
Judy Linard, Terry Woodley

KINGFISHER
An imprint of Kingfisher Publications Plc
New Penderel House, 283–288 High Holborn, London WC1V 7HZ

This edition first published by Kingfisher Publications Plc 1998
Originally published in France by Nathan
under the title *Megascope: Fascinants pharaons d'Egypt*

2 4 6 8 10 9 7 5 3 1

Copyright © Nathan, Kingfisher Publications Plc 1997
English text copyright © Kingfisher Publications Plc 1998

A CIP catalogue record for this book is available
from the British Library

ISBN 07534 0 222 X

· Printed in Italy

Postcard

The larger temple at Abu Simbel

This temple was carved out of a cliff face in Nubia. The front is decorated with four colossal statues of King Rameses II. In 1964, work started to move the whole temple to a higher spot to save it from being drowned by the waters of Lake Nasser, which was created when the Aswan Dam was built.

Postcard

Zoser's pyramid

Over 2,500 years old, the step pyramid was the inspiration of the wise man Imhotep. The pyramid symbolizes the palace in its enclosure, surrounded by offices and storerooms. But it actually contained King Zoser's tomb.

Postcard

Stela

A stela was like a gravestone. It recorded the names of the owner and his family, and listed all the offices he had held in life. It prayed for offerings to be made for him and his family for eternity.

Postcard

The papyrus plant

Papyrus grew in abundance in the marshes. It was used to make paper, mats, sandals, boats, roofs and many more things.

Stickers

Pepi I

Khufu

Gold mask of Tutankhamun

Model of a small boat

Model of a granary

Amosis

Senusret I

Alexander the great

Postcard

A day in the marshes

Hunting tasty wild ducks or catching delicious fish in the marshes was a pleasant pastime for a noble. He would take his family along and they would have a picnic and enjoy sailing on the river. This painting comes from the tomb of Nakht, dated 1410 BC.

Postcard

Khufu's pyramid

The Great Pyramid at Giza is one of the seven wonders of the ancient world.It once measured 147 m in height, but it has lost the topmost stones, so it is now only 136 m tall. It has a magnificent gallery leading to the King's Chamber, where the granite sarcophagus rests. There are no inscriptions in the pyramid at all.

Postcard

Sennedjem the workman

Sennedjem was one of the men who worked on the royal tombs.
He lived at Deir el-Medina and built himself a small but beautifully
decorated tomb there. In this wall painting from his tomb, Sennedjem
and his wife work in the fields in the Next World, surrounded by
lush vegetation.

Postcard

A troop of spearmen

This model of a troop of Middle Kingdom soldiers was found in a
noble's tomb. Armed with shields and spears, they march in some long-
forgotten parade. They were placed in the tomb to accompany
their owner's spirit into the Next World.

Postcard

The double crown

The pschent, as the ancient Egyptians called it, combined the Red Crown of Lower Egypt and the White Crown of Upper Egypt.

Postcard

The sarcophagus of Tutankhamun

The granite sarcophagus contained three, human-shaped coffins. Two were of wood, covered in gold and inlays. The third was solid gold. Inside was Tutankhamun's mummy, embalmed and bandaged, with a gold face-mask.

Postcard

Soldier in his chariot

In the New Kingdom, the Egyptian army introduced the chariot. Horses were foreign imports, so they were very valuable creatures and were well cared for. The light chariot usually carried a driver and a warrior.

Postcard

Protecting the king's name

'That which the sun encircles' – that is, the world – was represented in hieroglyphs by a cord with the ends tied together, in a cartouche. In Egyptian cartouche means 'protection'. The king's names (he had a personal name and a name as king) were always written inside a cartouche.

Stickers

Mummy of Rameses II

Cleopatra on a gold coin

One of Tutankhamun's necklaces

Papyrus

Cartouche
of a
pharaoh's
name

Cartouche of a
pharaoh's
name

A seated scribe, Dynasty XVIII

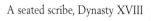

Mentuhotep

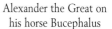

Alexander the Great on
his horse Bucephalus